The Maya Bechi Method

Raising Reliable Rebels Notebook

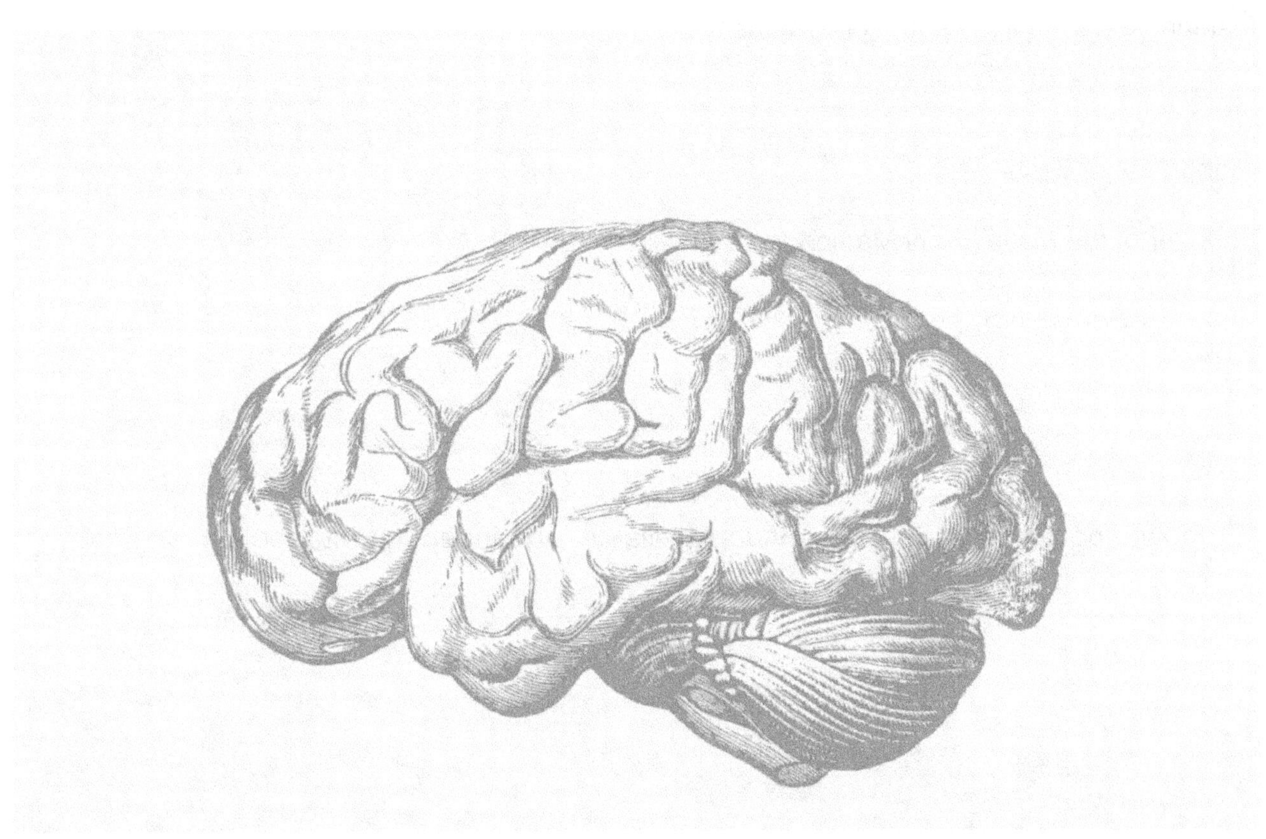

The Maya Bechi Method
Raising Reliable Rebels Notebook

Transform your approach to parenting with actionable strategies rooted in the E.A.S.E. tracker™, ANCHOR Plan™, and EMOTION Tip™. This workbook is designed to help you cultivate independence, resilience, and meaningful connections with your adolescent while fostering a harmonious home environment.

Author: Maya Bechi, M.Ed

Founder of the Maya Bechi Method™

"Empowering parents to raise confident, reliable, and independent rebels."

Published By:
Robson and Puritan Publications™
www.robsonandpuritan.com
contact@robsonandpuritan.com

© 2025 Maya Bechi. All Rights Reserved.

Introduction

Parenting adolescents in today's world has earned a hard locked reputation as a complex journey. Starting today, I want you to commit to the following:

We are going to drill it down to the bare basics and peel back the curtain on an anti-stereotype truth. Parenting adolescents is actually simple. Albeit not easy.

In your hands is a method that asks you to fully embrace the depth of your power in training and supporting your teenager and pre-teen.

NO MATTER HOW ILL EQUIPPED YOU MAY FEEL.

Raising Reliabel Rebels with The Maya Bechi Method™ (MBM) offers a comprehensive suite of frameworks designed to simplify the journey, empower families, and address modern parenting challenges with confidence. *Especially* during a time when you think that there is nothing more you can do but wait until age 18 arrives.

This workbook integrates three core frameworks: the **E.A.S.E. Tracker™**, the **ANCHOR Plan™**, and the **EMOTION Tip™**. Together, these tools provide a roadmap for fostering connection, resilience, and self-awareness within your family.

Maya Bechi
Texas

Section 1: Reclaiming Time and Energy with the E.A.S.E. tracker™

What is the E.A.S.E. tracker™?

The E.A.S.E. tracker™ (Evaluate, Align, Streamline, Enrich) is designed to help families assess commitments, streamline schedules, and create space for what truly matters. By reclaiming time and energy, families can focus on meaningful connections and shared growth.

How to Use This Framework

1. **Evaluate**: Assess the value of current commitments.
2. **Align**: Ensure activities align with family priorities.
3. **Streamline**: Eliminate or reduce time-consuming activities.
4. **Enrich**: Replace with restorative family-focused alternatives.

Worksheet

- **Activity Scoring Sheet**
- **Weekly Activity Tracker**
- **Reflection Prompts**

Templates for Implementing the E.A.S.E. tracker

Here are customizable tools to help evaluate and manage extracurricular activities while reclaiming time and energy in your family. These templates include a Scoring Worksheet for assessing activities, a Weekly Activity Tracker to monitor commitments, and a Reflection Worksheet for evaluating changes over time.

How to Use This Tool (4 copies of the E.A.S.E worksheet is included)

1. **Initial Assessment**: Use the **Scoring Worksheet** to evaluate all current extracurricular activities and identify potential adjustments.
2. **Weekly Monitoring**: Fill out the **Weekly Activity Tracker** to see how time is allocated and identify stressors or imbalances.

Ongoing Reflection: Complete the **Reflection Worksheet** monthly to assess progress and make iterative changes.

1.E.A.S.E. Scoring Worksheet

Purpose: Evaluate extracurricular activities to determine their alignment with your family's priorities and their impact on time and energy.

| **Activity Name**: ______________________ | **Date**: ______________________ |

Category	Question	Score (1–5)	Comment
Evaluate	Does this activity support academic growth, personal identity, or self-awareness?		
	Does my teen genuinely enjoy this activity, or do they feel obligated to participate?		
	How much time does this activity consume weekly (including travel and prep)?		
	What impact does this activity have on my teen's sleep, downtime, or mental health?		
Align	Does this activity offer opportunities for family involvement or bonding?		
	Does this activity contribute to my teen's sense of identity or long-term goals?		
Streamline	Can this activity be paused, reduced, or replaced with an alternative that better supports our family's priorities?		
Enrich	Could time spent on this activity be redirected to something restorative, like family bonding or individual growth?		

Scoring Key:

- **1**: Strongly Disagree
- **3**: Neutral
- **5**: Strongly Agree

Total Score: ______________________
Decision: Keep / Adjust / Pause

1.E.A.S.E. Scoring Worksheet

Purpose: Evaluate extracurricular activities to determine their alignment with your family's priorities and their impact on time and energy.

| **Activity Name**: ____________________ | **Date**: ____________________ |

Category	Question	Score (1–5)	Comment
Evaluate	Does this activity support academic growth, personal identity, or self-awareness?		
	Does my teen genuinely enjoy this activity, or do they feel obligated to participate?		
	How much time does this activity consume weekly (including travel and prep)?		
	What impact does this activity have on my teen's sleep, downtime, or mental health?		
Align	Does this activity offer opportunities for family involvement or bonding?		
	Does this activity contribute to my teen's sense of identity or long-term goals?		
Streamline	Can this activity be paused, reduced, or replaced with an alternative that better supports our family's priorities?		
Enrich	Could time spent on this activity be redirected to something restorative, like family bonding or individual growth?		

Scoring Key:

- **1**: Strongly Disagree
- **3**: Neutral
- **5**: Strongly Agree

Total Score: ____________________

Decision: Keep / Adjust / Pause

1.E.A.S.E. Scoring Worksheet

Purpose: Evaluate extracurricular activities to determine their alignment with your family's priorities and their impact on time and energy.

| **Activity Name**: _____________________ | **Date**: _____________________ |

Category	Question	Score (1–5)	Comment
Evaluate	Does this activity support academic growth, personal identity, or self-awareness?		
	Does my teen genuinely enjoy this activity, or do they feel obligated to participate?		
	How much time does this activity consume weekly (including travel and prep)?		
	What impact does this activity have on my teen's sleep, downtime, or mental health?		
Align	Does this activity offer opportunities for family involvement or bonding?		
	Does this activity contribute to my teen's sense of identity or long-term goals?		
Streamline	Can this activity be paused, reduced, or replaced with an alternative that better supports our family's priorities?		
Enrich	Could time spent on this activity be redirected to something restorative, like family bonding or individual growth?		

Scoring Key:

- **1**: Strongly Disagree
- **3**: Neutral
- **5**: Strongly Agree

Total Score: _____________________
Decision: Keep / Adjust / Pause

1.E.A.S.E. Scoring Worksheet

Purpose: Evaluate extracurricular activities to determine their alignment with your family's priorities and their impact on time and energy.

| Activity Name: _____________________ | Date: _____________________ |

Category	Question	Score (1–5)	Comment
Evaluate	Does this activity support academic growth, personal identity, or self-awareness?		
	Does my teen genuinely enjoy this activity, or do they feel obligated to participate?		
	How much time does this activity consume weekly (including travel and prep)?		
	What impact does this activity have on my teen's sleep, downtime, or mental health?		
Align	Does this activity offer opportunities for family involvement or bonding?		
	Does this activity contribute to my teen's sense of identity or long-term goals?		
Streamline	Can this activity be paused, reduced, or replaced with an alternative that better supports our family's priorities?		
Enrich	Could time spent on this activity be redirected to something restorative, like family bonding or individual growth?		

Scoring Key:

- **1**: Strongly Disagree
- **3**: Neutral
- **5**: Strongly Agree

Total Score: _____________________

Decision: Keep / Adjust / Pause

2. Weekly Activity Tracker

Purpose: Monitor weekly commitments and ensure alignment with family priorities.

| **Week of**: ___________________ |

Day	Activity/Commitment	Time Spent (hrs)	Family Involvement (Y/N)	Energy Impact (Low/Medium/High)	Note
Monday					
Tuesday					
Wednesday					
Thursday					
Friday					
Saturday					
Sunday					

Reflection:

- Which activities align most with our family priorities?
- Which commitments caused the most stress or required significant time?
- What changes can we make for next week?

2. Weekly Activity Tracker

Purpose: Monitor weekly commitments and ensure alignment with family priorities.

| **Week of**: ___________________ |

Day	Activity/Commitment	Time Spent (hrs)	Family Involvement (Y/N)	Energy Impact (Low/Medium/High)	Note
Monday					
Tuesday					
Wednesday					
Thursday					
Friday					
Saturday					
Sunday					

Reflection:

- Which activities align most with our family priorities?
- Which commitments caused the most stress or required significant time?
- What changes can we make for next week?

2. Weekly Activity Tracker

Purpose: Monitor weekly commitments and ensure alignment with family priorities.

| Week of: _____________________ |

Day	Activity/Commitment	Time Spent (hrs)	Family Involvement (Y/N)	Energy Impact (Low/Medium/High)	Note
Monday					
Tuesday					
Wednesday					
Thursday					
Friday					
Saturday					
Sunday					

Reflection:

- Which activities align most with our family priorities?
- Which commitments caused the most stress or required significant time?
- What changes can we make for next week?

2. Weekly Activity Tracker

Purpose: Monitor weekly commitments and ensure alignment with family priorities.

| Week of: _____________________ |

Day	Activity/Commitment	Time Spent (hrs)	Family Involvement (Y/N)	Energy Impact (Low/Medium/High)	Note
Monday					
Tuesday					
Wednesday					
Thursday					
Friday					
Saturday					
Sunday					

Reflection:

- Which activities align most with our family priorities?
- Which commitments caused the most stress or required significant time?
- What changes can we make for next week?

3. Reflection Worksheet

Purpose: Evaluate changes over time to assess the impact of adjustments on your family's time, energy, and connections.

| Reflection Date: _____________________ |

Category	Question	Your Reflections
Reclaiming Time	How has our schedule changed since making adjustments to extracurricular activities?	
	What new family activities or routines have we added to replace paused commitments?	
Reclaiming Energy	How has our family's overall energy level improved? Have we reduced stress or burnout?	
	Have collaborative household responsibilities eased the burden on parents and empowered teens?	
Family Dynamics	Have these changes strengthened our family bond?	
	How have these adjustments impacted communication and teamwork in our family?	
Teen Development	Is my teen showing improved self-awareness, sleep quality, or mental health?	
	Have they demonstrated greater responsibility or engagement in family life?	

Action Plan for Next Month:

- **Keep Doing**: What worked well and should continue?
- **Adjust**: What could be modified for better results?
- **Eliminate**: What isn't working and should be reconsidered?

3. Reflection Worksheet

Purpose: Evaluate changes over time to assess the impact of adjustments on your family's time, energy, and connections.

| Reflection Date: _____________________ |

Category	Question	Your Reflections
Reclaiming Time	How has our schedule changed since making adjustments to extracurricular activities?	
	What new family activities or routines have we added to replace paused commitments?	
Reclaiming Energy	How has our family's overall energy level improved? Have we reduced stress or burnout?	
	Have collaborative household responsibilities eased the burden on parents and empowered teens?	
Family Dynamics	Have these changes strengthened our family bond?	
	How have these adjustments impacted communication and teamwork in our family?	
Teen Development	Is my teen showing improved self-awareness, sleep quality, or mental health?	
	Have they demonstrated greater responsibility or engagement in family life?	

Action Plan for Next Month:

- **Keep Doing**: What worked well and should continue?
- **Adjust**: What could be modified for better results?
- **Eliminate**: What isn't working and should be reconsidered?

3. Reflection Worksheet

Purpose: Evaluate changes over time to assess the impact of adjustments on your family's time, energy, and connections.

| **Reflection Date**: _______________________ |

Category	Question	Your Reflections
Reclaiming Time	How has our schedule changed since making adjustments to extracurricular activities?	
	What new family activities or routines have we added to replace paused commitments?	
Reclaiming Energy	How has our family's overall energy level improved? Have we reduced stress or burnout?	
	Have collaborative household responsibilities eased the burden on parents and empowered teens?	
Family Dynamics	Have these changes strengthened our family bond?	
	How have these adjustments impacted communication and teamwork in our family?	
Teen Development	Is my teen showing improved self-awareness, sleep quality, or mental health?	
	Have they demonstrated greater responsibility or engagement in family life?	

Action Plan for Next Month:

- **Keep Doing**: What worked well and should continue?
- **Adjust**: What could be modified for better results?
- **Eliminate**: What isn't working and should be reconsidered?

3. Reflection Worksheet

Purpose: Evaluate changes over time to assess the impact of adjustments on your family's time, energy, and connections.

| **Reflection Date**: _____________________ |

Category	Question	Your Reflections
Reclaiming Time	How has our schedule changed since making adjustments to extracurricular activities?	
	What new family activities or routines have we added to replace paused commitments?	
Reclaiming Energy	How has our family's overall energy level improved? Have we reduced stress or burnout?	
	Have collaborative household responsibilities eased the burden on parents and empowered teens?	
Family Dynamics	Have these changes strengthened our family bond?	
	How have these adjustments impacted communication and teamwork in our family?	
Teen Development	Is my teen showing improved self-awareness, sleep quality, or mental health?	
	Have they demonstrated greater responsibility or engagement in family life?	

Action Plan for Next Month:

- **Keep Doing**: What worked well and should continue?
- **Adjust**: What could be modified for better results?
- **Eliminate**: What isn't working and should be reconsidered?

Section 2: Fostering Identity with the ANCHOR Plan™

What is the ANCHOR Plan™?

The ANCHOR Plan™ (Ask, Navigate, Co-Create, Hold Space, Offer Feedback, Reaffirm Autonomy) supports collaborative identity formation in adolescents. This process emphasizes mentorship and shared growth rather than hierarchical instruction.

How to Use This Framework

1. **Ask**: Encourage open-ended reflection about goals and values.
2. **Navigate**: Work through challenges collaboratively.
3. **Co-Create**: Establish rituals and routines that celebrate individuality.
4. **Hold Space**: Allow safe exploration of new ideas and interests.
5. **Offer Feedback**: Provide balanced guidance.
6. **Reaffirm Autonomy**: Empower adolescents by validating their choices.

Expanded Templates for the ANCHOR Plan

Below are detailed templates for using the ANCHOR process to address common family challenges including creative solutions for polarizing topics such as **social media use** and **differing political or social beliefs**. These templates guide parents and teens through collaborative identity anchoring while fostering mutual understanding and growth.

To gain a better understanding of what collaborative identity anchoring includes, please refer to the complete book: *Raising Reliable Rebels: The Maya Bechi Method*

Template 1: Addressing Social Media Use

Challenge: Balancing teens' desire for online connection with parents' concerns about screen time, privacy, and mental health.

1. **Ask Open-Ended Questions**
   - *"What do you enjoy most about social media?"*
   - *"How do you think your online presence reflects who you are?"*
2. **Navigate Challenges Together**
   - Present any realistic scenario: *"Imagine a friend posts something about you online that you didn't want shared. How would you handle it?"*
   - Discuss possible actions and their consequences, such as addressing the friend, reporting the post, or seeking support.
3. **Co-Create Rituals**
   - Establish family "digital detox" times, such as device-free meals or a weekly offline activity. Make these moments feel like opportunities for connection rather than restrictions.
   - Example: "Board Game Night" replaces an evening of scrolling, with teens choosing the game, the time and the duration, to empower their involvement.
4. **Hold Space for Exploration**
   - Encourage your teen to create content that reflects their passions, such as art, music, or causes they care about.
   - *"Would you like to share your creative side online in a way that inspires others? How might you do that?"*
5. **Offer Balanced Feedback**
   - Acknowledge efforts to use social media positively: *"I noticed you shared that post about environmental awareness. That was thoughtful and showed your values."*
6. **Reaffirm Autonomy**
   - Validate their decisions: *"You've taken steps to manage your time online and stay safe. How has that felt for you?"*

Outcome: The teen feels heard and empowered to make mindful choices about social media use while strengthening family connections through collaborative rituals.

Template 2: Navigating Differing Political or Social Beliefs

Challenge: Teens begin to form opinions that diverge from family values, leading to potential conflicts or misunderstandings.

1. **Ask Open-Ended Questions**
   - *"What sparked your interest in this topic?"*
   - *"How do you feel your beliefs align with your values?"*
2. **Navigate Challenges Together**
   - Present a "what if" scenario: *"Imagine a heated debate with someone who disagrees with your view. How would you approach that conversation?"*
   - Explore strategies like active listening, sharing personal perspectives calmly, or finding common ground.
3. **Co-Create Rituals**
   - Host regular "debate nights" where family members discuss a topic respectfully, with each person presenting their perspective and asking questions.
   - Example: Rotate topics such as climate change, voting, or school policies, ensuring the teen's topics are prioritized to encourage engagement.
4. **Hold Space for Exploration**
   - Encourage teens to research their beliefs independently while maintaining open dialogue.
   - *"What sources do you trust most on this topic, and why?"*
5. **Offer Balanced Feedback**
   - Focus on their thought process rather than agreement: *"I appreciate the way you explained your perspective. It shows you've thought deeply about this."*
6. **Reaffirm Autonomy**
   - Validate their growing independence: *"I respect that you're forming your own opinions. It's okay for us to see things differently as long as we keep listening to each other."*

Outcome: The teen gains confidence in their ability to articulate and refine their views while learning to engage respectfully with differing perspectives.

Template 3: Managing Household Responsibilities

Challenge: A teen resists participating in household tasks, leading to friction over shared responsibilities.

1. **Ask Open-Ended Questions**
   - *"What household task would you feel most comfortable taking responsibility for?"*
   - *"What do you think a fair division of responsibilities looks like in a family?"*
2. **Navigate Challenges Together**
   - Use a practical scenario: *"If the trash isn't taken out and it overflows, what's the best way to prevent that from happening again?"*
   - Discuss how shared responsibilities impact the family dynamic.
3. **Co-Create Rituals**
   - Introduce a "household swap" day where family members exchange tasks to appreciate each other's roles.
   - Example: The teen handles cooking for the day while a parent takes on a chore typically managed by the teen.
4. **Hold Space for Exploration**
   - Allow teens to experiment with managing a specific area of the household, such as meal planning or laundry, for a week.
   - *"What would it feel like to be in charge of this task for a week? What would you need to succeed?"*
5. **Offer Balanced Feedback**
   - Highlight effort and initiative: *"I saw how much thought you put into planning dinner. That was impressive!"*
6. **Reaffirm Autonomy**
   - Empower them with decision-making authority: *"It's up to you how to approach this task. I trust you to figure out what works best."*

Outcome: The teen learns the value of shared responsibilities while gaining independence and confidence in managing household tasks.

Template 4: Exploring Identity Through Hobbies and Interests

Challenge: A teen struggles to balance new hobbies with existing responsibilities or feels uncertain about trying something unfamiliar.

1. **Ask Open-Ended Questions**
   - *"What drew you to this new hobby?"*
   - *"How do you think this interest connects to your goals or values?"*
2. **Navigate Challenges Together**
   - Pose a scenario: *"What would you do if your hobby conflicted with a family responsibility, like a chore or event?"*
   - Brainstorm strategies for balancing priorities.
3. **Co-Create Rituals**
   - Celebrate the hobby by designating time for the family to support or participate.
   - Example: If the teen loves painting, hold a family art night where everyone creates something.
4. **Hold Space for Exploration**
   - Encourage trying out the hobby without fear of judgment or pressure to excel.
   - *"What do you enjoy most about this activity? Is there a part you'd like to explore further?"*
5. **Offer Balanced Feedback**
   - Focus on their passion and growth: *"You've really put effort into learning this skill. It's great to see how much you're enjoying it."*
6. **Reaffirm Autonomy**
   - Let them set their own goals: *"You decide how much time to dedicate to this. What feels manageable with everything else going on?"*

Outcome: The teen feels supported in pursuing their interests while learning to balance responsibilities and personal growth.

Summary

The ANCHOR Plan is flexible, allowing families to address diverse challenges collaboratively. By focusing on open dialogue, mutual respect, and shared experiences, parents and teens can navigate polarizing topics and everyday struggles while strengthening their relationships.

Section 3: Empowering Emotional Growth with the EMOTION Tip™

What is the EMOTION Tip™?

The EMOTION Blueprint™ (Explore, Map, Organize, Test, Interpret, Own) equips adolescents with tools for emotional self-awareness and regulation. This framework promotes resilience, self-reflection, and accountability.

How to Use This Framework

1. **Explore**: Identify and document emotions.
2. **Map**: Understand triggers and patterns.
3. **Organize**: Develop strategies for managing emotions.
4. **Test**: Experiment with solutions.
5. **Interpret**: Reflect on long-term patterns.
6. **Own**: Celebrate progress and identify areas for improvement.

Worksheet

- **Mood Journal Template**
- **Trigger Mapping Exercise**
- **Resilience Action Plan**

Innovative Framework:
The EMOTION TIP

The "EMOTION Tip" is designed to guide teens through a systematic process of emotional self-awareness and growth:

1. **Explore Feelings**: Encourage journaling or voice memos to identify and document emotions as they arise.
2. **Map Out Triggers**: Identify specific situations, environments, or interactions that cause emotional responses, both positive and negative.
3. **Organize Actions**: Develop actionable steps to manage emotions, such as practicing gratitude, setting boundaries, or using calming techniques like breathwork.
4. **Test Solutions**: Experiment with different coping strategies and seek feedback from trusted family members or peers.
5. **Interpret Long-Term Patterns**: Reflect on recurring emotional patterns to understand deeper triggers and responses.
6. **Own Growth**: Regularly assess successes and challenges in emotional regulation, celebrating progress and identifying areas for improvement.

Tools and Resources

To support this process, introduce practical tools such as:

- **Emotion prompts**: Cards with prompts for identifying and articulating feelings.
- **Mood Journals**: Structured notebooks with sections for recording emotions, triggers, and coping strategies.
- **Apps**: Technology like mindfulness or mood-tracking apps designed for adolescents to self-monitor their emotional states.

Activities: Co-Participating in Emotional Growth

Inspired by Family-Based Emotional Interventions
Studies, such as those from the **Journal of Family Psychology**, emphasize that co-participation in activities strengthens family bonds and emotional regulation. Building on this research, emotional growth activities are designed to include family members while keeping the adolescent's self-discovery at the forefront.

Refined Activities

- **Cultural Recipes**: Cooking specific family or cultural dishes together fosters emotional connection and reinforces a sense of heritage and identity.
- **Family or Cultural Dance**: Engaging in shared physical activities, like salsa or a traditional cultural dance, releases endorphins and builds trust through synchronized movement.
- **Meditation and Breathwork**: Co-practice techniques like guided meditations or the "box breathing" method, which calms the nervous system and models healthy emotional regulation.
- **Replace One Community Activity with Family Time**: Swap an external event (e.g., a sports practice) for a family outing where open discussions about emotional growth are encouraged.

Activities: Triggering Positive Hormones and Bonding

The Science Behind Hormonal Responses

Building on research about oxytocin (the "bonding hormone") and dopamine (associated with reward and pleasure), intentional activities can foster emotional resilience and strengthen relationships. Shared moments of vulnerability and success trigger these positive hormones, making emotional regulation a shared journey.

Activities to Trigger Bonding Hormones

1. **Cooking and Eating Together**: Sharing meals prepared collaboratively enhances oxytocin levels, particularly when the meal holds personal or cultural significance.
2. **Heart-Centered Practices**: Use heart intelligence techniques like synchronized breathing while holding a calming or affirming thought, which can reduce stress and promote connection.
3. **Collaborative Gratitude Practice**: End the day with each family member sharing one thing they are grateful for, which enhances dopamine and promotes positive emotional habits.

Activities: Practical Steps to Build Emotional Resilience

Inspired by Cognitive Behavioral Techniques
CBT focuses on identifying negative thought patterns and replacing them with healthier ones. Adapted for adolescents, the following steps integrate self-awareness with practical, action-based techniques:

1. **Identify Emotional Triggers**: Work together to pinpoint situations that consistently cause stress or frustration.
2. **Set Emotional Goals**: Encourage teens to identify a specific emotional skill they want to improve (e.g., patience, managing anxiety).
3. **Create a Coping Toolbox**: Develop a personalized "toolbox" of strategies, such as listening to music, taking a walk, or practicing visualization.
4. **Role-Play Scenarios**: Simulate challenging situations, like a disagreement with a friend, and brainstorm responses that align with their emotional goals.
5. **Reflect and Adjust**: Schedule regular check-ins to discuss what strategies worked and what didn't, fostering adaptability and continuous growth.

How This Approach Differs from Existing Practices

While traditional emotional education often relies on structured therapy or teacher-led activities, this approach integrates family involvement, cultural practices, and independent tools. It also focuses on real-world application, where teens actively practice and reflect on their emotional regulation strategies rather than passively learning about them.

Unique Contributions

- The **EMOTION Tip** provides a clear, step-by-step framework for self-directed emotional growth, emphasizing ownership and adaptability.
- Family-focused activities like cultural cooking or dancing enhance bonding while respecting and reinforcing heritage.
- Practical tools like mood journals or apps allow for continuous, independent engagement in emotional growth.

By embedding these practices into daily life, teens not only develop emotional resilience but also learn to integrate their emotions into their broader sense of identity and purpose.

Section 4: Practical Applications for Your Home

Tailoring MBM to Your Home Dynamics

- **Two-Lead Adult Homes**: Strategies for collaboration and teamwork.
    - Adjust scenarios, stories and any other activity by including your personal experiences.
    - Set aside time to pre-read or play with an activity together first.
- **Extended or Blended Families**: Tips for celebrating diversity and managing complexity
    - Intentionally choose to give lead roles to the teen who has expressed feeling left out in previous conversations. Then allow them to choose who will lead next.
    - Partner teen to lead a parent with whom there has been the more frequent needs for adapting to styles.
- **Single Parent or Independent Youth Homes**: Ideas for empowering teens and sharing responsibilities.
    - Use these worksheets independently
    - Keep and share the results and your answers on these pages at meetings and decision making environments to advocate for yourself and your needs.

Dealing with Resistance

- Strategies for addressing pushback.
    - Give 2 options, or 3 options with a pre-set time limit for when activity will end
    - Honor agreed upon time limits. Be rigid with this.
    - Make participation non-negotiable for a duration of time, provide a hiatus, then resume with activities in a second phase with a limited duration of time.
    - Building trust and an ability to predict when they can escape the activity will build trust.
- Staying consistent despite challenges.
- Build with patience and persistence.

Reflection Questions

1. What challenges does your family face with current routines or responsibilities?
2. Which framework feels most aligned with your immediate needs?
3. How can your family work together to implement these changes?

Conclusion

The Maya Bechi Method™ Workbook provides practical, actionable steps for navigating parenting and adolescent development. With the E.A.S.E. Framework™, the ANCHOR Process™, and the EMOTION Blueprint™, families can reclaim time, foster identity, and empower emotional growth. Use this workbook to create lasting connections and prepare your adolescents for success.
